Joshua
I0756108

Dedicated to my wonderful children and grandbabies. May they always lean on the One who walks with them continuously.

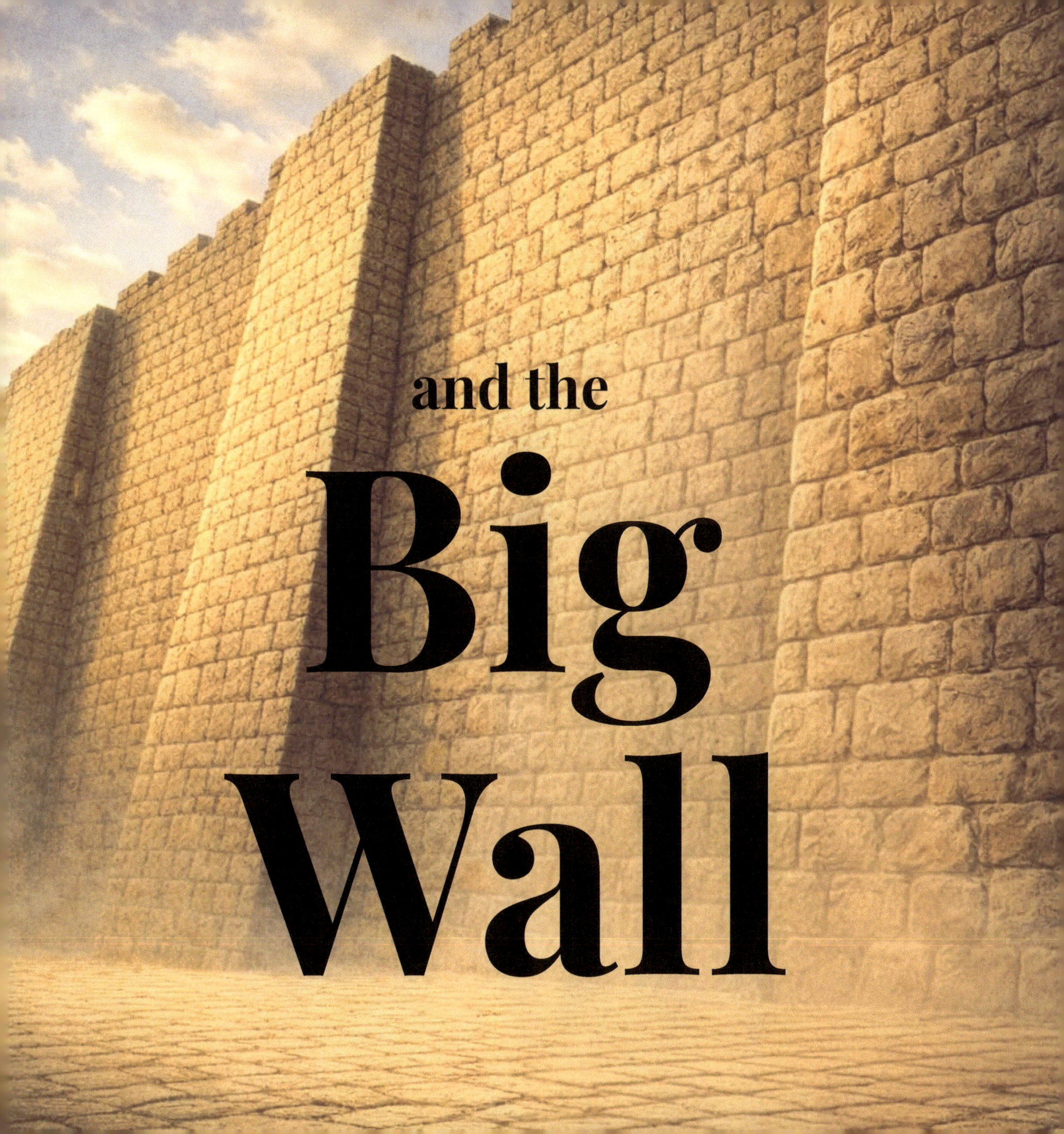
and the
Big
Wall

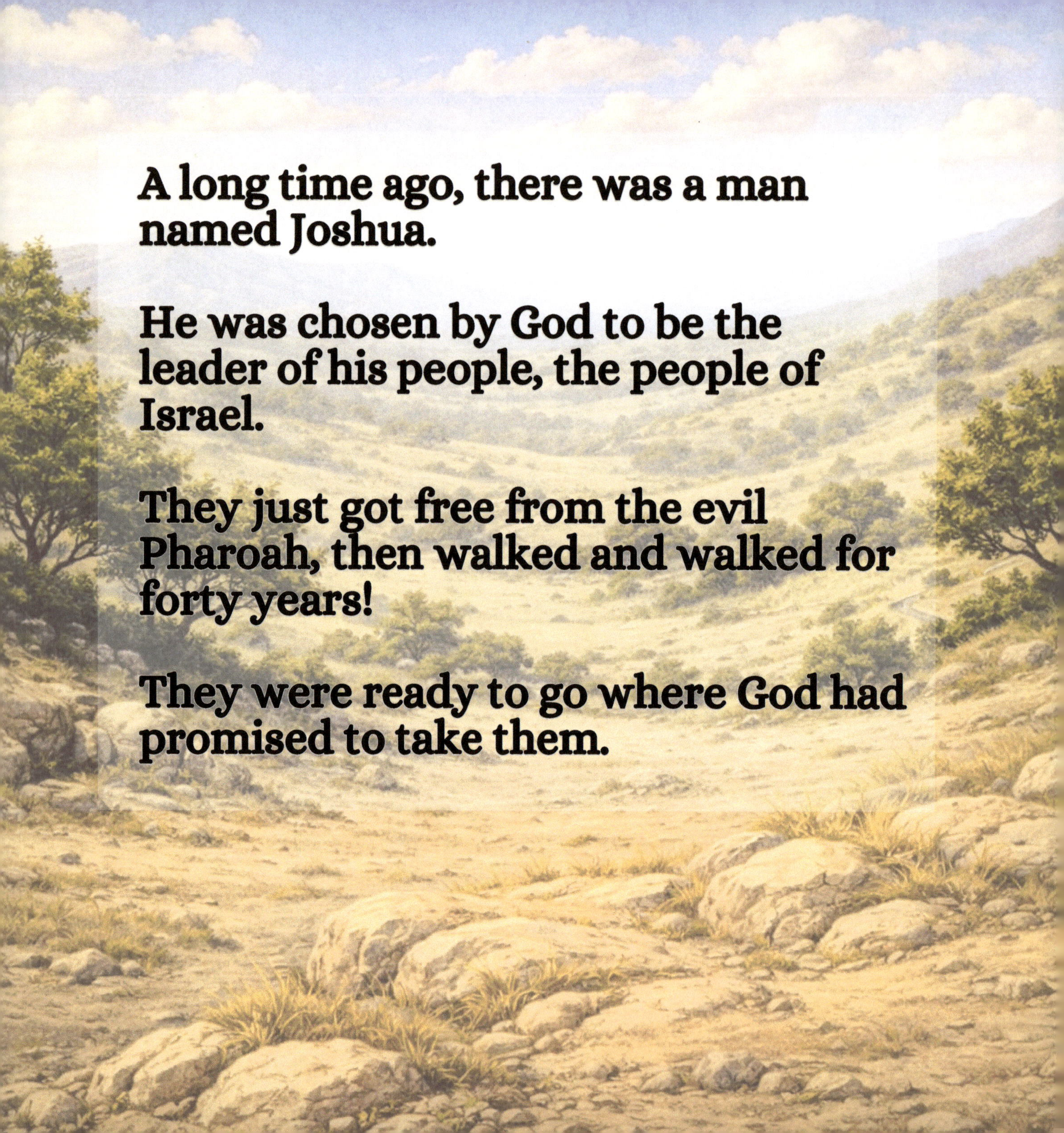

A long time ago, there was a man named Joshua.

He was chosen by God to be the leader of his people, the people of Israel.

They just got free from the evil Pharoah, then walked and walked for forty years!

They were ready to go where God had promised to take them.

One day, God told Joshua, "It's time to go to the land I'm giving you! You will have to face many hard and scary things; but don't be afraid. I will always be there with you. Be strong and brave. I am your God, I will help you wherever you go."

Joshua knew that God always kept His promises, so he listened to what God was saying.

Before they left, Joshua sent out two spies. He wanted them to see how the land and the people were. Especially a big city called Jericho.

He knew that God promised He would give them the land. But he also knew it had really big walls to protect it.

While in Jericho, the two spies were almost caught. But a brave woman named Rahab hid them.

To thank her for protecting them, they promised to protect her and her family when they came to take her city.

They told her to tie a red rope from her window so they would know which place to keep safe and not destroy.

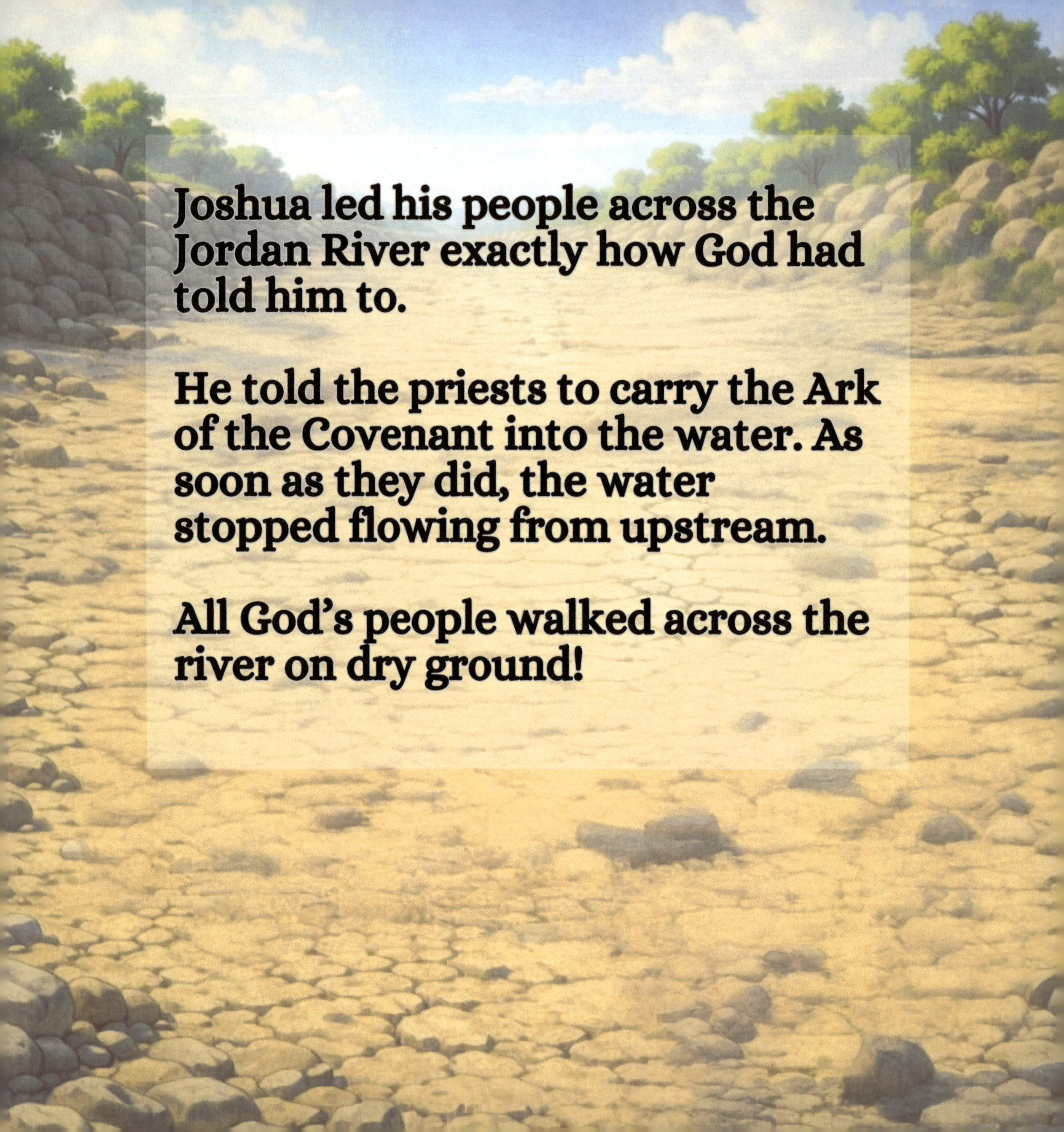

Joshua led his people across the Jordan River exactly how God had told him to.

He told the priests to carry the Ark of the Covenant into the water. As soon as they did, the water stopped flowing from upstream.

All God's people walked across the river on dry ground!

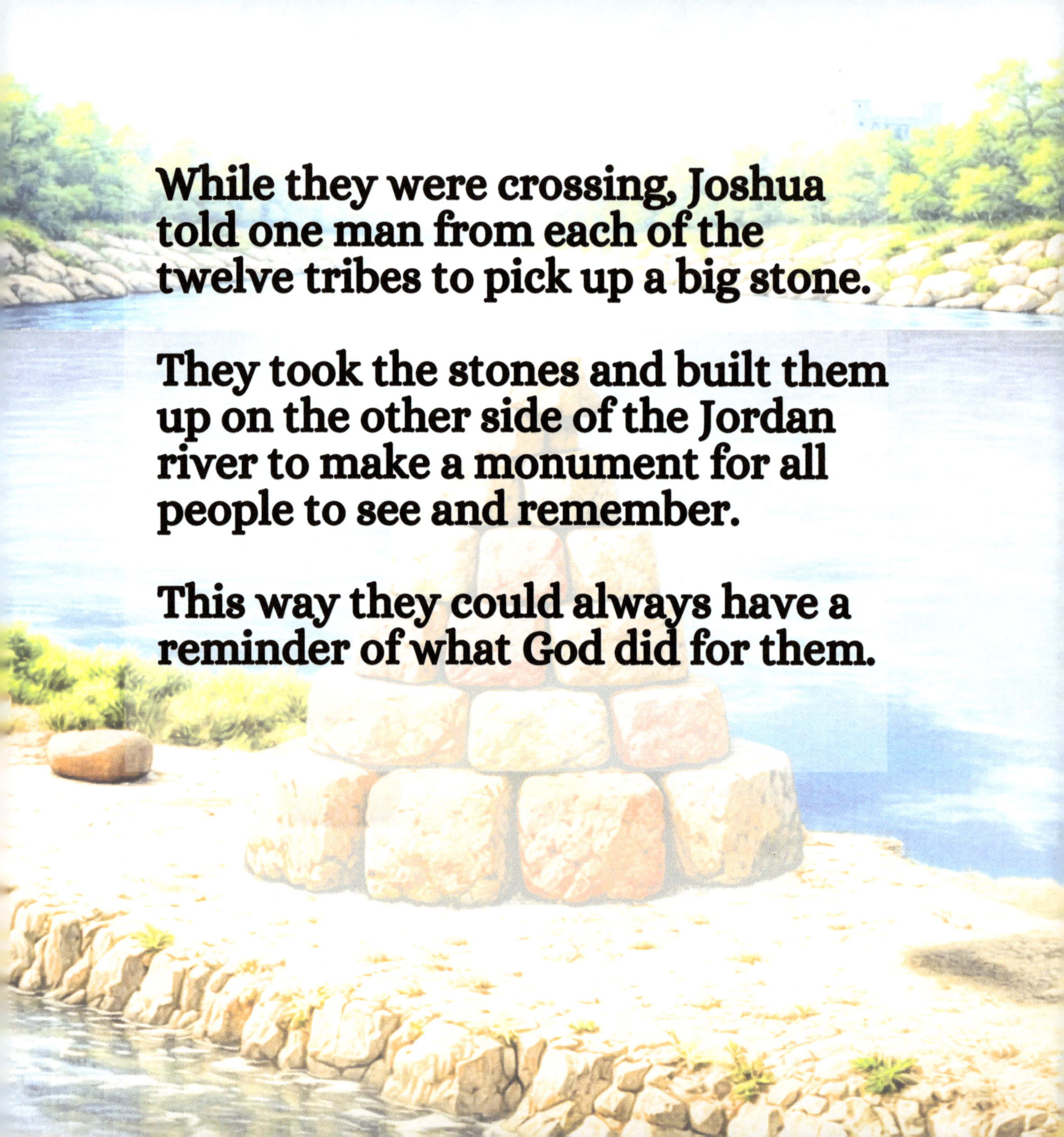

While they were crossing, Joshua told one man from each of the twelve tribes to pick up a big stone.

They took the stones and built them up on the other side of the Jordan river to make a monument for all people to see and remember.

This way they could always have a reminder of what God did for them.

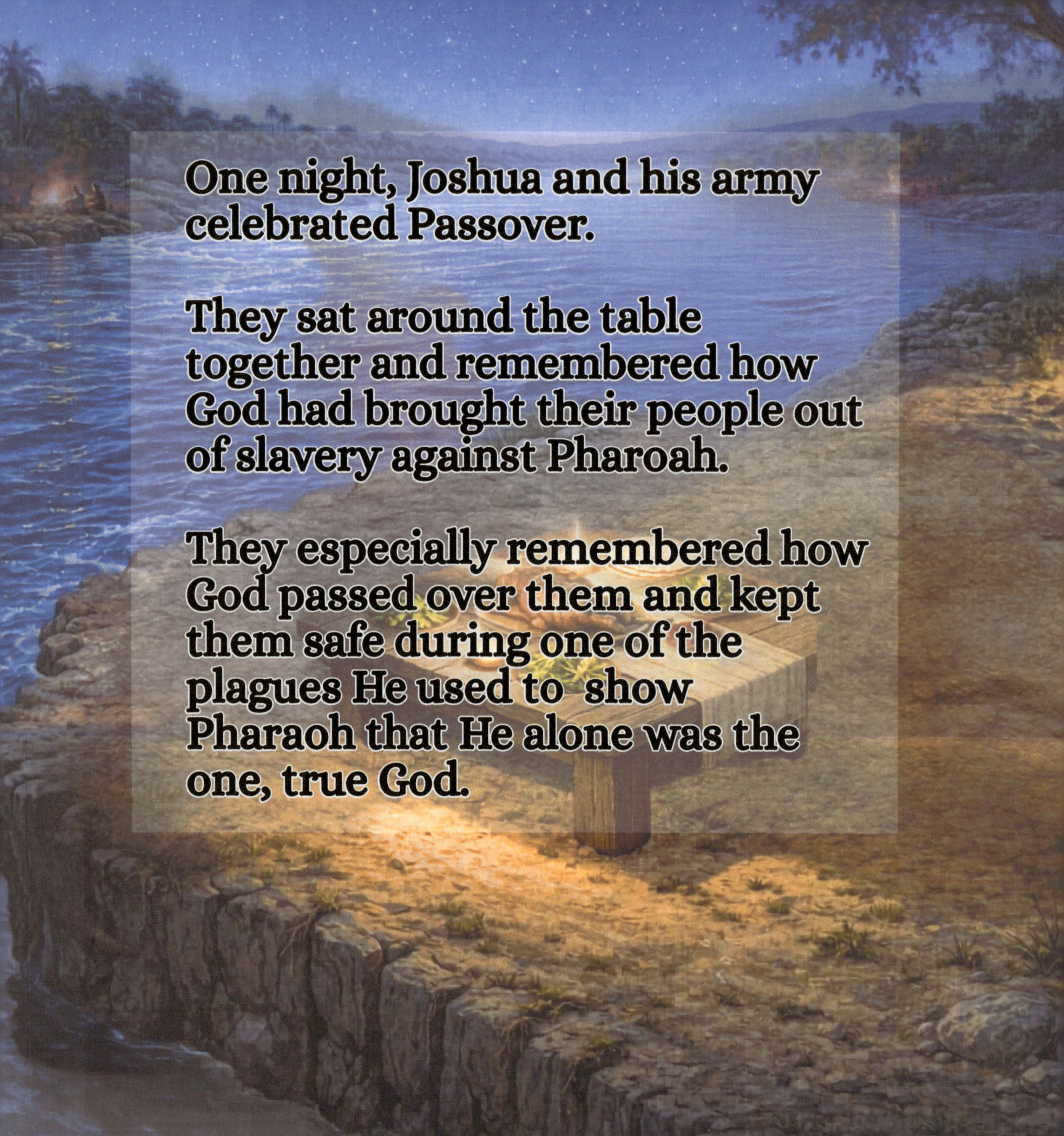

One night, Joshua and his army celebrated Passover.

They sat around the table together and remembered how God had brought their people out of slavery against Pharoah.

They especially remembered how God passed over them and kept them safe during one of the plagues He used to show Pharaoh that He alone was the one, true God.

Soon they came upon the city of Jericho. It had really big walls to protect its people from other armies. The people who lived there were afraid when they saw the people of Israel nearby. They locked all of their gates and wouldn't let anyone leave or come in.

They thought they were safe.

But Joshua told the Israelites what God's plan was.

Joshua told them that they had to march around the city walls one time every day for six days without shouting the battle cry, or yelling, or even talking.

They had to just march around the city following the Ark of the Covenant.

It didn't make sense to them, but they knew they had to do what God told them to.

Then on the seventh day, they walked around the city seven times.

But this time something was different.

After the seventh time around, they weren’t quiet. The priests blew their trumpets and the Israelites all shouted as loud as they could.

And the walls started to fall!

When the walls fell down flat, the Israelite soldiers went in and took the city and everything in it, just like God told them to do.

They destroyed everything except one place, the place that had the red rope on it.

That place was marked as a place of safety for Rahab and her family because of her service to God's people.

Joshua gave praise to God for all the promises that He kept.

In your life, if you have something that seems too big for you, never forget that you have a God who is bigger.

Trust in Him and listen to what He says. He will always be there for you and guide you.

Be brave and strong!

www.ingramcontent.com/pod-product-compliance
Lightning Source LLC
LaVergne TN
LVHW070208110826
845147LV00002B/532

9781955678247